Conversations with My Self

I dedicate this little book of poems to

Jeannie,

Cathy Cesnik

&

Survivors of child sexual abuse

"At 15, life had taught me undeniably that surrender, in its place, was as honorable as resistance, especially if one had no choice."

Maya Angelou

Introduction

My healing journey as a clergy sexual abuse survivor who repressed my memory of the experiences has been my life's work. For many years, journal writing has been a major part of that process. Journaling is a powerful tool for self-exploration and expression. I find it to be painfully insightful, so at times I partner with a therapist. The practice of journaling continues to be extremely helpful as I journey to remember and reconnect with my younger self.

In 2009 I sat down to write a book, hoping to share my journey with others, and found myself paralyzed by the blank page. Out of the pressure to write came some of these poems. I added others I had written through the years. This free flow form of writing became a doorway for that part of myself I had left behind to communicate with the present day me.

These pure conversations with my teen self can be disturbingly raw and painful to read. I feel that when I read them! I however was deeply changed touching the depth of pain and suffering my younger self was sharing with me. It was a level of feeling I had been afraid to enter into. I could not separate my teen self from my present self in that horrible pain. There was no room for pretense. She was me! It will be impossible for me to ever again diminish the dehumanizing, torturous raping of my body, mind and spirit by others.

I have learned over the years to discern where my inner journey takes me. I believe I can tell the truth of my experiences by the fruits they bear. The fruits of this process have consistently been juicy, sweet and nourishing. Out of the terrible pain I share through these poems came a deeper understanding, acceptance and level of personal wholeness within my Self.

Carl Jung, a Swiss psychiatrist whose ideas are the basis of Jungian psychology, believed, "The self is not only the centre but also the whole circumference which embraces both conscious and unconscious..." (from Psychology and Alchemy) Working with all aspects of my personality, conscious and unconscious, continues to bring me a deeper sense of peace with my Self which is what I'm always aspiring to.

I hope you find these poems, and the practice of journaling, helpful tools as you journey along your path to health and wholeness. May we all find comfort and strength knowing we are not alone!

-Jean Hargadon Wehner

TABLE OF CONTENTS

*   Graphic Content – may be triggering for survivors

Conversations with My Self:

A Collection of Poems

by

Jean Hargadon Wehner

A New Beginning – Easter 1992

Studies completed, office prepared, clients scheduled

ready to finally step out in my life!

Paralyzed by a wall of terror,

standing on the edge of darkness,

at the door to the Chaplain's office.

Confused and fear-filled

I do not want to be here.

Why am I here?

From deep within my Self I hear,

"If you want to move out in your life you must go in this room."

I try to say, "No!"

I cannot stop Truth from penetrating the fear.

I open the door.

Walking into pure darkness

I stand on the edge of hell's abyss.

Doubting all that has brought me to this moment

I feel totally alone.

I wait…

and so it begins.

NO MORE

I hear me through the stillness

shouting, "I am silenced."

screaming, "I am silenced."

crying out, "I am silenced NO MORE!

I will have my say

Silent <u>NO</u> <u>MORE</u>!"

"And I have the firm belief in this now…that when you follow your bliss, doors will open where you would not have thought there were going to be doors and where there wouldn't be a door for anybody else."

Joseph Campbell

Buried Alive

During one of the more intense times of my healing process I had a very powerful meditation. It continued over the course of weeks.

A woman stood barefoot, hair loose, stocky in form, wearing a long dress and apron. She was staring intently at the rocky side of a mountain. Her arms were outstretched. As days turned into weeks I not only saw her but also sensed her. She was staring so hard that light was pouring from her eyes and hands toward the rocks. It seemed to penetrate the surface.

At some point I found myself scratching and clawing through the rock, toward the light. I had been buried alive and the light was drawing me, helping me find my way out. I broke the surface and shielded my eyes from the brilliant light.

As I turned my head toward the tunnel of darkness, which led to my tomb, I saw many pairs of eyes staring up at me. There were others still down there!

January 1999

(Visual depiction of this can be found on The Keepers Impact website- www.thekeepersimpact.com)

Is It Too Late?

The time to speak out has not passed.
I cannot believe that it is too late.
Do not even try to say that to me.
I will not listen.
I will persevere
to find the right time to speak out.

I believe it is too late.
No one really cares.
It feels hopeless.
It seems senseless.
I don't think anyone will hear.
I don't think anyone will listen.

I will speak out anyway.
I will say what needs to be said.
I will let my voice be heard.
I will speak my truth.
I believe it is not hopeless.
Hope is all I have left.
Hope is what keeps me pursuing
the avenue of expression.

My hope has faded.
My trust in justice has been destroyed.
I'm not sure justice even exists.
It is not about truth.
It is not about justice.
It is about power and money.
It is about keeping the truth buried...secret.

I will speak out about the injustice.
I will speak the truth.
I will speak with
real power behind me.
I need to believe it will make a difference.
I need you to help me.
No need to believe.
Just help me,
Please!

I have said my yes.
My heart is not in it,
my head nods yes.
I really do not believe it matters.
It is too late.

"In the end, we will remember not the words of our enemies, but the silence of our friends."

Martin Luther King, Jr.

Who Is to Blame?

Is it the little girl innocently sitting on her uncle's lap,
or the young woman believing in God?
Possibly the adolescent shunned for becoming a woman,
or the nun trying to make a difference?
Maybe the teenager trusting God,
or the naive woman courageously confronting?
Could it be the abused teen locked up within her own mind,
or the parents who did their best, but did not know?
Or…
What of the God that allowed this horror,
the man who orchestrated such torture,
or the countless others who participated?
What of the community that turned a blind eye,
or the Church that believed they could bury the truth and it would
never surface?
No…
No blame to be found for them.
No blame to be owned and repented for by them.
The innocent carry the blame.

Forgive Myself

I forgive myself

I forgive myself for…
What others did to me.
What others made me feel like.
What others made me believe.
What others made me do.
What I did to survive.

I forgive myself

I forgive myself for…
Being afraid~
Being afraid~
Being afraid~
Being afraid~
when I needed to be strong
for me.

I forgive myself for being human!

Essence

Down in the dungeon
of my bowels,
chained to a wall,
iron collar around the neck,
attached to the chain,
attached to the wall.
No room to move.
Locked behind bars
with a guard at the door.

At first it is
hard to tell if it is
animal or human.

Ruby jewel plugging up
the mouth with
eyes and ears grown shut.
Hunched over,
dirty, scaly and
deathly still.

"Open the door!" I cry.
Guard replies, "No."
"She gave me the key
and said no one was
to be let in,
or out."

The Key

The key is…

secret.

Only a few know

the secret.

Only a few hold

the key.

Hold the key!

Keep the key!

Just *show me*

what the secret is

it keeps!

"The most potent muse of all is our own inner child."

Stephen Nachmanovitch

Reflection in a Mirror

I look in the mirror and see a sinner.
What can I do to make it better?

Stop throwing up.
Stop looking like
I don't like
what they are doing to me.
Trust he is protecting me,
standing by the door.

Looking in the mirror
I must see a whore.
He is trying to help me,
he is trying to guide me to be good.
I'm just a sinner.
Will I ever be forgiven?

I've done it again.
We look in the mirror,
he sees fear.
It is no wonder he has to punish me,
I am such a sinner.

Holy Spirit *

It is put on my head,

on my forehead.

What is it?

The Holy Spirit!

What does it do?

Cleans my soul.

Who told you that?

The priest.

Why do you let them?

I am a sinner and need forgiveness.

When will that happen?

"Soon," they say. "Real soon."

Do you believe them?

Priests don't lie.

They help us stop lying.

What do you do with

the Holy Spirit?

Leave it there through the day.

What do they do?

Watch me leave with it on my forehead

and smile.

It will be soon!

Soon *

Smells so strong
they make me dizzy.
Don't throw up,
please don't throw up!
The pressure at the back of my throat
makes me gag.
Don't throw up,
please don't throw up!
The taste of skin and pee
upsets my stomach.
Don't throw up,
please don't throw up!
The Holy Spirit filling my mouth,
makes me want to spit.
Don't throw up,
please don't throw up!
My head hurts,
My mouth isn't mine anymore.
I swallow the Holy Spirit
then
look to see if I am forgiven.
"Soon," he says. "Real soon."

Redemption *

I am in the room of redemption.
I hope this time
I will be forgiven.

It must be a terrible thing I did,
to have the forgiveness of God
take so many months…years?
I think I am going to hell
if I don't get it right this time.

In and out
mouth
no thinking of smells, DON'T throw up.
Great!
That is what he is looking for.
Smile,
don't look scared.
Good!
That is what he is looking for.
I think I will be forgiven
today.

Am I Here?

I am here.
It is clear.
Feel the pull of hair.
I must be here.
Feel the strain of the pull.
Look at the face
raging into mine,
contorted and spitting.
No yelling, just raging.
I am here.
I must be here.
Why can't I feel my feet
on the ground?
Am I here?

"Courage
doesn't always roar.
Sometimes courage is
the quiet voice at
the end of the day
saying
I will try again tomorrow."

Mary Anne Radmacher

Eyes of Jelly

As I sit by the chair
I look with eyes
that do not see.
I have fooled them again.
They think they are
looking at me.
Little do they know
I am not even there.
I've left quite
some time ago.
My eyes are just
empty pools of jelly
trying not to be found out.
If they knew
they would eat them too.

The Collar *

It is red and colorful.
I am aware of how
soft it is.

It fits my neck like it was
made for it.
The madras material
on the inside
keeps it from
cutting or chafing
my neck.

As the buckle is fastened
I leave the room.

I can see the leash now being connected.
Poor thing,
It is a shame
she needs to go through
that treatment.
She has been told,
time and time again,
it is for her own good.

I am glad the collar
is so soft!

The Gun *

The gun is
on the table.
The table is between him and me.
The gun is
on the table.
Then it is in his hands.
I look at the gun.

Do I see him?
Do I see anything but the gun?
I see the bullets,
one by one,
removed and placed
on the table.
One then the other,
until all six are
on the table.

What does he look like?
Is he even there?
The gun is small and dark grey,
the holes empty.
The gun is held by a hand
next to my head.
It feels cold.

Is he speaking?
I can't hear anything
over the deafening sound
of the click of the trigger.

Holy Water *

I am alone
sitting in my sanctuary.
In the confounds of this sacred space
I am safe within this cupboard,
no one around.
I can breathe the
stale air.
I can hide behind the bucket
and
stare into the filthy dirty old water.
I can pretend
the smell of dirty mop in sour water
is all I really smell.
The stench on my own body
is covered over
by this saving water,
washing my senses clean.

Silent Scream *

Lying on a table,
feet in stirrups,
legs apart.

Pain screams through me!
When did I get on this table?
The pain brings me back.
Blood warm on my leg.

Standing, "STAND UP!"
Pot in hands,
legs apart.

Something falling
out of the painful scream
into the pot.

Someone, far away
calls it candy.
It doesn't look like
candy.

Why am I here?

"GOD
grant me the
SERENITY
to accept the things I cannot change,
COURAGE
to change the things I can, and
WISDOM
to know the difference."

Reinhold Niebuhr

Responsible

When...When...When...
did I become responsible?

Forced into submission through
humiliation, embarrassment, guilt and shame.
Terrified, hit, yelled at and threatened
Forced into believing I made everything in
the Room
happen, every detail.

When did I go from being
manipulated and forced,
to believing I was
the orchestrator of the actions in
the Room?

When did I stop knowing
he was making everything happen,
and begin thinking
I was responsible for everything happening?

Continuing to fear that whatever I do or say,
makes me responsible
for everyone else's actions,
is my living out
the Room
over and *over* and *over* again!

"One does not become enlightened by imagining figures of light, but by making the darkness conscious."

C. G. Jung

Mirror, Mirror Who do I See?

I think I know who I see

while gazing in the mirror

at this face I call

Me.

"Don't dare look too close or too long, but look."

Whose eyes are they?

Whose mouth is that?

I think I know, do I?

I should not look too closely, but do.

Those eyes belong to one who knows

the Truth.

They *scare* Me...

NO - DO NOT STARE!

It's not polite.

I'm a good girl.

But, what might I see

while staring into those eyes of Truth?

A power-filled Me

who shatters the mirror

destroying…

Me?!

Don't look too close or too long.

That's a good girl.

In Memory of Cathy Cesnik

1942 – 1969

How Was I to Know?

(for Cathy)

If it weren't for her,
I wouldn't be here.
If she had stayed quiet,
I wouldn't be here.
If she intended to leave me in the dark,
I wouldn't be here.

I wanted her to leave me alone!
I wanted her to mind her own business!
I wanted her to save me…

How was I to know I was her business?

Too intense after she left.
They were so afraid of the light,
"Stomp out every ember!"
Nothing left to do
go deep, deep, deep
within.

How was I to know,
the depth would save me?
How was I to know, if it weren't for her
I wouldn't be here.

39

"The eyes are the window to your soul."

William Shakespeare

"Don't look too long or too deep, but look."

"Look me in the eyes.
Let me see how much you like this.
Look me in the eyes!"

What do I see?
Fear
~~~crazy~~~
Anger

What do I see?
A man who is,
Crazy Scared
Crazy Mad
Crazy Powerful

I see eyes that say,
"I see you and will tell others
if you say what you see
in me."
Eyes that SCREAM,
"I will kill you if you say a word!"
Eyes that whisper, *"You are just like me - you like this."*

I know you.
I looked you in the eyes and I saw you.
I was told not to look too long or too deep,
but <u>you</u> made me look
D E E P
and I saw you!

In memory of Ethel Tarun Hargadon

1927 – 2016

Also known as:
Ess, Mom, Grandmom,
GG, Aunt Ess

I experienced deep peace with my mom before she died.
She was not to blame!

Where Were You?

Tiny and frail…Lost in a bed of pillows and "stuff".

"1, 2, 3 up…I got you.

Turn, turn, turn…are you on the pot?"

"You need your nourishment, build energy, that's it, sleep."

Where were you?

He said you'd disown me.

He said you'd throw me away,

"Out on the street!"

Why couldn't you see beyond my wall of fear?

So much distance, anger and longing

Even as I change you, bathe you, feed you

I feel the wall he created between us.

Each brick a lie, a betrayal, deliberate and connived.

I know it the same as

I know you're not asleep, just too tired to hold your eyelids open.

Yet as I still stand behind this wall I ask,

Where were you?

Would you have discarded me like these half-used

tissues and straws?

Would you have believed his lies?

How could you not, I did.

We'll never know, we'll never know…

Turning you on your side, your leg is stiff and sore.

Heating pad, Tylenol, sleep

You can't leave me!

How can you leave me standing behind this wall yelling,

Where were you?

Dedication to Mike Wehner

1950 - 2007

Who is This Man

Who is this man who sits before me weary and frail?
This man lacking of hair and tooth and the muscles we once
knew.

Who is this man?

This man is the young buck who galloped into my life
and saw the Me I couldn't even imagine, determined to have this
"hard-headed woman" in his life. Savior comes to mind.

This man is the husband who only knew he loved me, and that
was enough. Who helped me trust the sacred act of loving and
believe in its power.

Who is this man who sits before me scared and real?

This man is the father who stood by his first born, helpless and
powerless to help. Gently encouraging and coaxing me to touch,
coo, stroke and whisper, then name our son not Edward Brent but
Mathew Eric!

Who is this man?

This man is the spiritual companion who always felt okay with his
concept of God, no matter how it changed in my life – God the
Father, Great Mother, unfamiliar voices, churches/groups,
spiritual explosions.

Who is this man who feels like 'a fish out of water',
unable to help another for lack of physical strength,
build something, move something, re-create
or better yet create something?

This man is the strongest man I know. He was my eyes when I
couldn't see. He was my legs when I couldn't walk. He was my
protective shield when I was at my most vulnerable. He was my
fist when I didn't even know I had hands. He believed I was good
when everything in me screamed HARLOT!

This man who sits before me is…

Husband, who still believes that his love for me is all that matters.
Father, who loves his children more than anything!
Grandfather, who has the basketball, glove and ball safely
waiting. Father-in-law, who values his daughter-in-law and all she
brings to the family.

Friend, who values that he can be depended upon while
questioning his worth to others. Surprised and touched by loved-
one's outpour of well-wishes and expressions of how he touches
them.

This man Mike is my soul mate. The man I love through sickness
and in health, through richer or poorer

-forever.

Let Go

So much to hold onto,
so little energy left.
How do I go on with such emptiness?
I must let go.

How do I let go of love,
disappointment, fear, anger?
Let go of dreams,
yet dream of being more.
Let go to what?
Just do it!
Easier said than done.

Let go of the unspoken
feeling that life is over and
love found is now lost,
needing to see in order to believe
that life and love go on.

Let go
of the paralyzing
thought that I
must let go.

Enough…
No more thoughts of letting go.
I will embrace the heartache and pain,
learn to accept loss as part of
life shared with
those I love.

"One of the most calming and powerful actions you can do to intervene in a stormy world is to stand up and show your soul. Soul on deck shines like gold in dark times. The light of the soul throws sparks, can send up flares, builds signal fires, causes proper matters to catch fire. To display the lantern of soul in shadowy times like these—to be fierce and to show mercy toward others; both are acts of bravery and greatest necessity."

from "You Were Made For This"
by Clarissa Pinkola Estes

Resources:

If you need help or information…

1.)   The Body Keeps the Score
       Brain, Mind and Body in the Healing of Trauma
               by Bessel Van der Kolk, MD

2.)   Memories, Dreams, Reflections by Carl Jung

3.)   The Keepers Social Impact Site
       http://thekeepersimpact.com/

4.)   RAINN https://www.rainn.org/

       hotline: 800-656-4673 (24/7)

5.)   How do I journal?
       http://www.tmswiki.org/ppd/How_do_I_journal%3F

Made in the USA
Columbia, SC
31 December 2017